MAKING ~ WAVES

MAKING ～ WAVES

emma j. sykes

GARNET PRESS

Copyright © 2019

All rights reserved.

This book or part thereof may not be reproduced in any form, stored in a retrieval system, or transmitted in any form by any means-electronic, mechanical, photocopy, recording, or otherwise without prior written permission of the publisher, except as provided by United States of America copyright law.

The information provided in this book is designed to provide helpful information on the subjects discussed. This book is not meant to be used, nor should it be used, to diagnose or treat any medical condition. The author and publisher are not responsible for any specific health needs that may require medical supervision and are not liable for any damages or negative consequences from any treatment, action, application, or preparation, to any person reading or following the information in this book.

References are provided for information purposes only and do not constitute endorsement of any websites or other sources. In the event you use any of the information in this book for yourself, the author and the publisher assume no responsibility for your actions.

Making Waves
Emma J. Sykes

Tradepaper ISBN: 978-1-945026-56-0

Library of Congress Control Number: 2019940141

Published by Sacred Stories Publishing
Printed in the United States of America

to all those searching,

all those dreaming,

and all those already there

TABLE OF CONTENTS

I Unknown Potential..1

II Moving With Darkness...13

III Have Courage And Fly..25

IV Here We Are Witness..35

V Never Silence Us...47

VI Let's Take A Journey...61

VII The Final Chapter..73

Meet Emma 97

I sit here in silence
With no thoughts in my head
Seeing a poem
Which only lays dead
Because of the fear,
The struggle, the pain,
To allow anyone
To even know my name.
And the persona I choose
Lies close to my heart
As a way to protect
The fire destined to start
The fire that burns
Every bridge in my soul
Sealing the approval
Of my ultimate goal.
Freedom to ride
On the waves painted black
With choices so endless
You never look back

I see the elements
As they live within me
And the 'Mother' as she returns
And continues to be
My greatest teacher,
In times such as these
When life becomes
A little more than a breeze.
But to all my Mothers,
As we continue to grow
I ask for your guidance
In this world down below
To ignite the flames,
The passion, the power,
To rise within me,
The Great Purple Flower.

I

Unknown Potential

In a world fraught with fear

and so

We begin

The blessing of our time
And the miracle in the madness
Is one so fraught
In this world of defective gladness

Where the ones who look
Slightly further than the eye
Are deemed an imperfection
From those who hide in the lie

For we shall not see the one
Who roams in the fields
Free from the conditioning
The manipulation, and the shield

And he calls to us
In our hearts and in our mind
But unless we find the courage
We will always stay completely blind

And as his mother waves goodbye
As he continues down his path
She knows this little boy
Will never hold an inch of wrath

Because he embodies freedom
In every single way
And he is not afraid
To take a risk for each new day

And that is what I'm saying
When I write these words out now
Never be afraid
To take your final bow

To open up your eyes
To the world of infinite dreams
Because believe me when I say
It's not as scary as it seems

But you have to be willing
To jump from the highest point
To be reborn again
To stand and anoint

Tell me please,
What's wrong with me?
I'm unable to cross life's rolling sea.

Beyond the rocky pillars of time
I float amongst the sludge and the grime,

And I cannot tell you

Why I must be,
The one to venture out to sea

But destiny awaits in us all my friends
And I will see it out until it all ends

Until all the walls come crumbling down
Until nothing is left but dust on the ground

Because I refuse to accept anything less than my truth
I play the drums and I sound the crwth

Can you hear it?

The place it beats in your heart

Yes there it is,

The fire destined to start.

The raptures rise
With fear in their eyes
Of the storms first appearance
In the dark, gloomy skies
And sitting beside them
On the rugged grey rocks
I ask them to sing,
A song from the docks
Of peace and tranquility,
And love in their heart
When they felt so alive
The entire Earth could part
But they'd still feel the wholeness
From the love they now knew
Like a new-planted tree,
It grew and it grew
And as they sang,
I looked to the skies
And saw it change
In front of my eyes

From the dark, gloomy clouds
Which lingered with dread
To a golden light,
Haloed in red
And I look to the raptures
Who lay silent now
And promise them
That I will seal my vow
To always sing
In my times of great pain
And wait for the sun
To beam through the rain.

Alone.
In a space, in a place,
Filled with all the hustle
The riot, the sickening noise of laughter
The place of death.
The place of sleep.
The place of destruction,
Where those who weep,
Shed light onto their demons.

Blinkered, blinded by some fake reality
Which at its best seems 'cool'
This place will be our death.
Poisoning our every orifice.

Deeming us to purgatory
And a life sentence in hell
It is the cycle not yet broken.
The temptation that leads us to evil.
Only at the gates will we realise the flaws of this reality

How it decayed us and left us for dead,
With nothing but a shell of reflection

In the rhythm of life
There's the soul that can't win
Every milestone causes an ache within

And through the tests and traumas
The sadness and sorrow
There's the chance of happiness waiting tomorrow

This soul waits and he waits
Within the four boxed walls
With nothing to fight for except his own cause

But what does he do?
He lies in his bed,
Waiting for something to fill his head

Because at the moment it's empty
Apart from the voice
Which rings in his ears that he must make the choice

But this he can't stand,
It brings him to anger
The message so clear he would rather hang… and

What can I say?
Except that 'I'm sorry'
For the brother I lost
And within a hurry,

Its over.

The speeches,
And the fancy brocade
Are distant memories and for some they fade

Into small specs of dust,
Which account for nothing
And they continue with life always rushing
With their 9-5 job, and the kids they've been pushing… but

For others it lingers
The heartache and dread
Of being left alone with no thoughts in your head

Left with the voice which causes the pain
The voice of yourself
I don't need to explain.

Writing the apology
Is the worst of them all
When you feel like you're standing
Waiting to fall
Into the abyss of
Blackness and dust
Where nothing remains
Apart from the lust
And the memory you have
Of where it went wrong
The feeling of weakness,
And no way to be strong
And I try to be kind,
Always. I promise.
But sometimes I see a side to me,
And to be honest,

I'm sad.

Because I don't mean to cause

Heartache and pain,
Like I've said time before,
I still search for my name.
But I guess we all must
Make our mistakes,
In order to evolve
As the human race
But I want you to know,
As I should have said at the start,
I'm sorry if I caused
Any pain in your heart,
And I'll always be here
To stand by your side,
As we both begin this
Long bumpy ride

Through life as we know it.

Plastered with red,
I'll sit here now,

Content in my head,
That I made the right choice
To write my truth out
As a way to dismiss
Any niggling doubt
About who resides
At the core of my heart
The girl with the fire
Destined to start

III

HAVE COURAGE, AND
FLY
THAT'S WHAT I WAS TOLD
TO DO

HAVE COURAGE.
ALWAYS

i sit and wonder
when it will be
that the stars shine brighter,
in this world for me
and although you may think
that's a 'rich choice of words'
believe me my friend,
we all go unheard
you see the problem with me
resides in my heart,
there's a part of my life
waiting to start
and I know what you're thinking,
i live in a bubble
but my world isn't filled
with heartache and rubble
i come from a place,
with distance from here
but you don't understand that,
do you My Dear?

and I'm sorry for you,
because if you'd have known
you were the one
i could have called my own

but we all have a journey,
a path and a voice,
and for us maybe,
it was the right choice
to sit here in silence
with hearts that once beated,
knowing that we
can rise undefeated.

if we glisten

on the purple deck

do we surrender

to a force which displaces stillness

or do we gain the right

to understand why the blue waves crash

against the surface of a buoyant water

because the classified isn't what we perceive

the glory isn't righteous

and the belief isn't real

so if I choose to take the midnight train

i'll see you in the New World

Two worlds collide
Universes meeting for the first time
We see, we hear, we acknowledge

We look.
But do we see
We hear.
But do we listen

I reach for you
Hands blazing with an energy beyond our control
Do you lift it with me?
Or choose another path
Are you afraid of seeing the unimaginable?

I am cut, broken and shattered
Yet I am fixable
I am the embers of the fire they thought had burnt out
I am the dreamer and the achiever
I am patient and kind

I am fearless, yet I am fearful
I contract and I expand

I am the star that shines the brightest
Yet I am unknown
I do not belong to any group or formation, I am not labeled or deriven
The only name I hold is the entity that I am
A star.

Born, survived but only recognised when dead.
That however is the illusion of me.
In my death I am seen and recognised, analysed and structuralised
I am not these things.

I am fire.
I am the flames that singe the skin
I am powerful and I am strong
I am unlike what anyone perceives

I can love though, I can laugh
I am unlike anyone else I know

The heart is unrelenting.

IV

HERE WE ARE WITNESS TO THE STORY WE BECOME AND THE VOICE WE HEAR

In my life

I've seen a lot of things

From world disasters

To promised kings

I've seen it all

At such a young age

And with eyes wide open

I'm free from the cage

I didn't decide

To follow convention

A life of being hemmed in

Would have only caused tension

And through following my heart

I found within me

A pool of talent

I never thought I would see

And it's hard to write
These praiseful words
But I have to fly high
So I can be with the birds

Because freedom is all
I've ever wanted in life
Disregarding all
The pain and the strife

I needed it more
Than anything else
So I could rise up above
And be as one with myself

the river of dreams
flows straight through my spine
keeping me upright
blooming roses and vine

the moon it rises
in the central brow
pulsating the energy
which awakens me now

and my hair it flows
like the rippling waves
of the tides, and the currents
and the sunsets on bays

in my eyes
the stars glint with the light
of a million memories
of the day and the night

and also with me
come the scratches and scars
of a lifetime of living
free from the bars

free from the boxes
brimmed with the rim
that dictates who can get out
and who can get in

the Earth it neutralizes
at the core of my heart
keeping me grounded
for each new start

and the fire it burns
through each living cell
pushing me forward
with my stories to tell

each of these things
make up who I am
the formula of life
without the exam

slipping into the abyss,
the blue water and the weightless dream,
the feeling of falling, sinking, dying,
the uncontrollable silence
the need to neither accomplish or fail
the drowning,
the uncontrollable ecstasy of drowning

immortality.

the blue glow and the black box,
the wall of stars and the dust waiting to be born.
the fusion, the fire, the creation
is that not what we dream of?
the starboard and the gateway to endless possibility

the mundane will be destroyed.

as a new pathway is forming
an army approaching

the Earth's children,

born of Poseidon, Hephaestus and Astraea,

the world is changing,

and the Battle soon won.

V

NEVER SILENCE US

OUR WORDS CUT DEEPER THAN KNIVES

WE STAND TOGETHER

I pay my respects
To the men who fell
In the war-torn scenes
That we paint so well

To the women
Who nursed, and kept the wheels spinning
Who always stood strong
From the beginning

To the animals
So patient, that fought by our side
Who didn't run
Who didn't hide

I pay my respects
As I think of you
In the massacre of madness
Demanding what's due

You fought to eradicate
The wars of your time
But I'm sorry to tell you
The conflict spread beyond crime

It manifests
On such a big scale
And lives within
Each fairytale

We have become a nation
Fraught with the fear
That if we speak up
We cannot live here

This world we've created
And called it 'free-land'
Yeah right, Okay…
Whose head is next in the sand?

It's lies man, it's riddled
It's what we've become
We're all so caught up
In all the hum-drum

It lives on today
And what we decide
Will impact the future
The next to reside

And when we all die
What will be left?
A will of hatred
Deals, and theft

Left to those
Who can't take it no more
Who truly want freedom
To let their heart soar

We have to fight back
Just as you did
To put the down the cheque
And place the bid

To be bold in our statements
And fight against power
To honour you
In your final hour

I know you wanted
Peace for our land
So you stood by your brothers
To lend a hand

I'm sorry we've let you down
In this way
But what I can truly,
Honestly, say

Is we are trying
Some of us, yes, it's a few
But I know we'll succeed
In what we've told you we'll do

Because we aren't afraid
Of the 'power' above
Let it rain down
We'll show them the love.

I appeal to the people
To really hear these words
I need you to promise me
I will be heard
We are living a life
Of deceit and lies
Spoon-fed these falsities
So the Elite can rise

Pardon me,
I am wrong.

They are not the 'Elite'
They are a corrupt minority
That claim they own Gods seat
Well I'm sorry,
I can't stand it
To sit here a mute
Knowing there isn't a single dispute
Over the torture,

The pain,

The hardships,

They cause

And nobody is taking a moment to pause

And ask why we are continuing

Our day-to-day lives

With not a question in this world

This world of great size

Anyway, moving on,

Before I cut all ties,

You know what I'm struggling with

What I really despise

The fact that they keep taking and taking from Earth

Living their lives of unorthodox mirth

Seeing themselves as the ultimate power

Who keep the 'scum' locked in the tower

But I'm telling you now

The tower will fall.

And when it does

They'll run.

They'll run from us all.

The double standards of men
And the way they speak
About a woman's choice
And the path she seeks
Causes pain in my heart
And anger in my soul
It ignites a fire that demands
I won't pay the toll
The charge.
The pittance.
The coins,
For being me
When I make my mistakes
I'm just learning you see
But you don't
You're so quick
To point out the blame
To spread round the lies
And ridicule my name
And it hurts because,

I stand as one with myself
With no one beside me
I'm left on the shelf
But it's fine.
I forgive you.
I know why you've said
The words that cause me
Undying dread
But I can never forget
That because you're a man
It's okay for you
To have disregard
For who I am.

VI

let's take a journey TOGETHER THROUGH EACH NEW DAY Speaking FOR OUR TRUTH

Let me tell you a story
One of a few
That began in my early years
Let's say 2002

I was dressed up smart
And sent off to school
To begin my journey
To gain the greatest tool

Education.

And this is where I saw them
The brown paper walls
Ladened with rules
And faces hidden in shawls

Faces with nothing
Not an inch of the passion
For the life they've been granted

Just dead in a fashion

And I became numb
With the lessons I'd been taught
Don't you be different
Don't you have thought
For anything else.

But I wasn't good
At the English or Maths
Or Science or Writing
Or recalling
The past,
The present
Or knowing each cloud in the sky
I thought I may as well wave the future good-bye

And this is why
The system must change
We need to re-define

And re-arrange

The way we see
Each child's potential
We need to grow as a nation
Now this is essential.

Completely, Totally, Proud of You
Said who?
The mask in the mirror
That only acts on a queue
Because you're not really,
If you're honest with me
You're only playing you're part and pretending to be
So you can get your gold star at the end of the day
And hear the praiseful chatter which deems you're okay.
But why pretend?
When you don't even know…

Who I am.

I forgive you though
And I understand why you struggle to see
The reason I've chosen this way to be me
And I pray for you
Because you've taught me so much
You've opened my eyes to why we need a touch…

Of magic.

And that's what I'm here to bring
To encourage the tiniest of flames to sing
Because we need it
In this time of hierarchal pain
To take back our rights and reclaim our name
And that's what I'm doing with my life when you ask
I'm fulfilling my ultimate God given task
So please don't tell me that you're proud of me
Until it comes from a place of sincerity.

Last night I witnessed death
In all its pale colours
And the faintness of the breath
And the way the face drained
As the spirit slipped away
To re-join the Kingdom
Of workers hard at play

But let this celebration
Be a witness for us all
To make sure we live our lives
Before we get the call

To re-join our friends and family
In Gods open skies
Before we make transition
To our ultimate demise

And I saw it in this man
The peace now in his heart

As he began the beginning
Of this beautiful new start

And with his son beside him
As he took his final breath
The room filled with light
In this peaceful time of death

And it's okay to mourn and weep
Over times spent together
But remember he is one with you
Like a bird and its feather

And now it's time to unite
As one with each other
And move forward down our own paths
Remembering our Brother.

VII

THE FINAL
CHAPTER
HERE UNITED
TOGETHER
KNOWING WE
CAN DREAM

If ship wrecks were to happen
As they often do
Would you still sing with me?
Or flee to someone who…
Could provide you with the silence
Of lovers after dusk
To fill the empty void
With nothing more than lust

And as you disappear,
I watch a can float by
Bobbing up and down
Under the beautiful blue sky
And as I think of you
As the can floats away
I remember all the memories
Of that bleak and dreary day
When you told me the sail had struck
And the ship had gone astray

And now I sit and wonder
As you ponder on your choice
Why I wait around
When I was given my own voice
To go and find my own new ship
One of perfect stature
So I can sing upon the decks again
With heaps of joy and laughter

To my Mother
Whose heart is as pure as gold
I write you this verse
Before it gets cold
Before the storms come
And tear this world down
Until there is nothing
But hope to be found
I want you to know
You've shaped how I've grown
And helped plant the seeds
That need to be sewn
You've risen me up
In times of great fear
And always been there
To combat the tears
You're a star in this world
With a light to be shone
And I know you won't stop
Until the suffering is gone

And this is why
I sit here with pride
Knowing that
I have you by my side
And together we can do it
Follow our dreams
And see the sun shine
In all its great beams
That's you Mum,
The Sun
It needs you to know
You're a messenger in this world
Our world down below
You've come to save millions,
Billions from pain
So they can see the light
And rise once again.

I have nothing left to write.

No more stories
No more fight
No more endless trepidation
Or monsters in the night

No more fire burning souls
Or starry painted skies
No more looking to the future
To our ultimate demise

No more walks along the street
With strangers in the night
No more counting out the days
Until I take passage on loves flight

No more ships that will set sail
From the harbour of my mind
No more lonely monologues

Or memories left to find
No more dealing with the lies
The apologies, the tears
No more looking at myself
And facing all the fears

No more searching for the happiness
Or speaking for our Mother
No more reading out the will
Or listening for our Brother

For now I have to leave you
Alone with my heart
Whilst I begin my next chapter
And go back to the start.

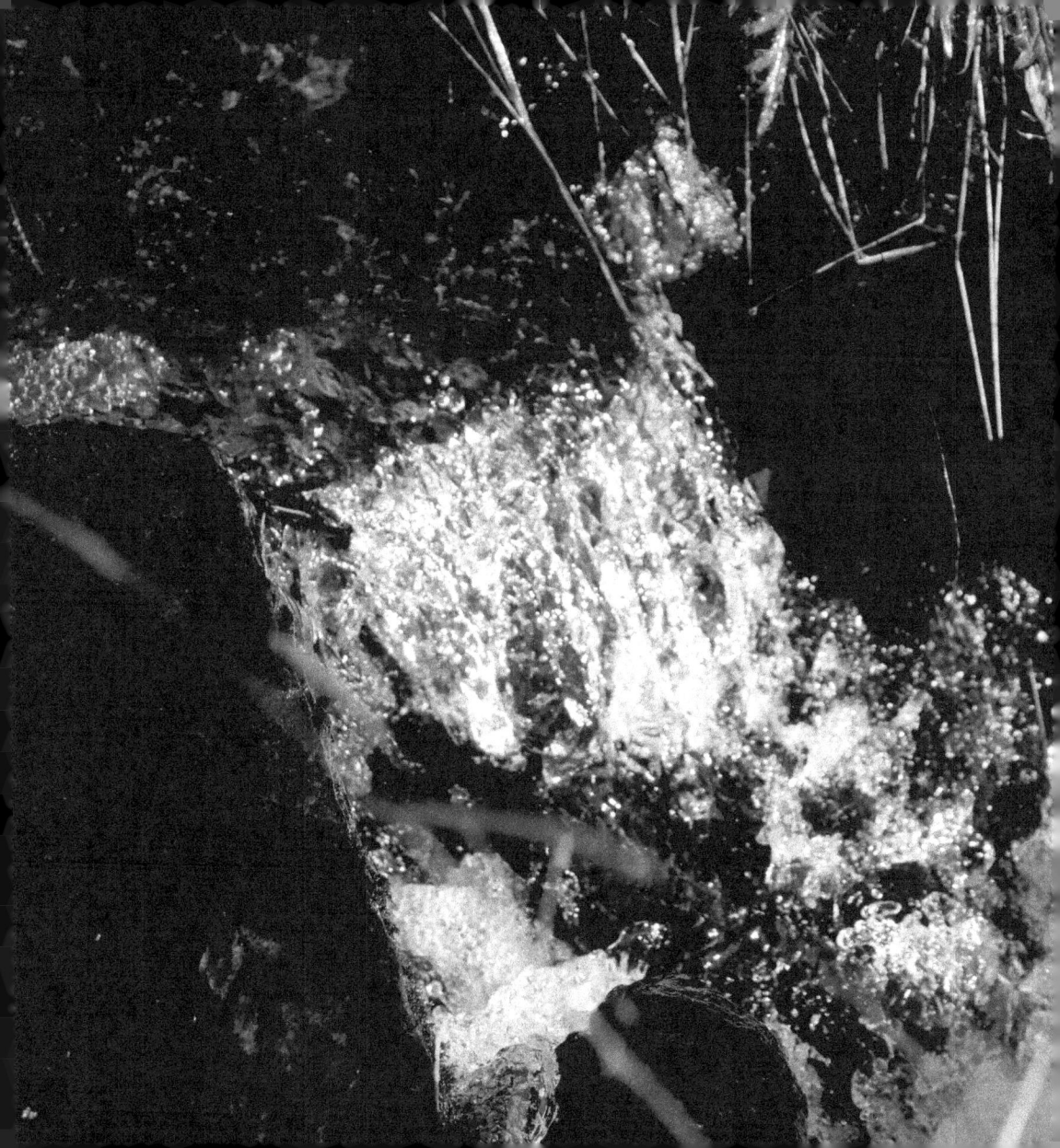

MEET EMMA

Emma's journey of writing began whilst she was training at Double Edge Theatre, Massachusetts, USA as a performer in the fall of 2017. The physicality of the training combined with the silence that it offered opened up space to freely express emotions and journaling quickly became a routine part of the creative process. As the training delved deeper, she found the writing became more elaborate and began to stray from documentation into a more poetic style.

After leaving the theatre and returning home her style developed and she started writing more lyrically basing many of the poems on experiences from her own life and those of lives close to her. She returned to the theatre in June 2018 for a further three months and wrote the opening poem of the book after participating in the Art and Survival scheme that the theatre hosts.

She returned back to the UK and continued to involve herself with shows, writing on the side as a hobby. On the 1st October 2018 she witnessed her stepfathers father pass away and wrote a poem that she read out at his funeral. She decided to put all her poems into a book to share with people her journey of Making Waves over the past two years and the freedom of expression that poetry opened up for her.

This is her story of turning fear into fearlessness and ripples into waves.

www.ingramcontent.com/pod-product-compliance
Lightning Source LLC
Chambersburg PA
CBHW080027130526
44591CB00037B/2691